Sch

Just the Facts
Cyber Crime
Neil McIntosh

www.heinemann.co.uk
Visit our website to find out more information about **Heinemann Library** books.

To order:
☎ Phone 44 (0) 1865 888066
🖹 Send a fax to 44 (0) 1865 314091
🖥 Visit the Heinemann Bookshop at www.heinemann.co.uk to browse our catalogue and order online.

Produced by Monkey Puzzle Media Ltd, Gissing's Farm,
Fressingfield, Suffolk IP21 5SH, UK

First published in Great Britain by Heinemann Library,
Halley Court, Jordan Hill, Oxford OX2 8EJ, part of
Harcourt Education. Heinemann is a registered
trademark of Harcourt Education Ltd.

Editorial: Nick Hunter and Jennifer Tubbs
Series design: Mayer Media
Book design: Jane Hawkins
Production: Viv Hichens

Originated by Dot Gradations Ltd
Printed and bound in Hong Kong, China by
South China Printers

ISBN 0 431 16144 5

06 05 04 03 02
10 9 8 7 6 5 4 3 2 1

British Library Cataloguing in Publication Data
McIntosh, Neil
  Cyber crime. - (Just the facts)
  1.Computer crimes - Juvenile literature
  I. Title
  364.1'68

Acknowledgements
The publishers would like to thank the following for
permission to reproduce photographs:
Associated Press 12 (Gene J Puskar), 14, 15 (ABC
News), 17 (Ed Wray), 18 (Jim Cole), 19 (Damien
Dovarganes), 20, 29 (Koji Sasahara), 31 (Ron
Edmonds), 32, 34, 36 (Toby Talbot), 37 (Daymon J
Hartley), 38 (Ted S Warren), 39 (Ted S Warren), 40
(Shizio Kambayashi), 43 (William Philpott); Corbis 9
(Henry Diltz), 24, 26, 28, 46, 50; Corbis StockMarket
22 (Ariel Skelley); Digital Vision 34-35; Kobal Collection
45 (MGM/UA); Popperfoto 8, 10 (Reuters), 13
(Reuters), 16 (Reuters), 21 (Reuters), 32 (Reuters); Rex
Features 6; Science Photo Library 7 (Sam Odgen); Still
Pictures 5 (Mark Edwards); Tim Mayer 49.

Cover photograph reproduced with permission of
Photodisk.

Every effort has been made to contact copyright holders
of any material reproduced in this book. Any omissions
will be rectified in subsequent printings if notice is given
to the publishers.

Any words appearing in the text in bold, **like this**, are
explained in the Glossary.

Contents

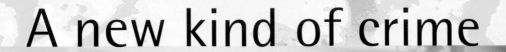

A new kind of crime

What do you think about when somebody mentions crime? It is easy to imagine crime just as we see it in movies: masked gunmen breaking into a building at night and stealing gold from under the noses of sleeping security guards, followed by a big car chase. Of course, in the end the police catch up with the bad guys and make an arrest, and the rule of law is restored.

However, there is a new kind of crime that is not so easy to see. There are no dramatic raids, no shoot-outs and no rubber masks. This is a world where the 'bad guy' can be thousands of miles from his victim. This is cyber crime: crime carried out using computers.

Using computers doesn't make it any less serious than 'real world' crime – huge amounts of money can be stolen, big businesses can be brought to a halt and illegal information can be swapped. It does mean, however, that criminals can live far away from their targets, and never leave their bedrooms to commit their crimes.

How does cyber crime happen?

Everyone knows that computers are very important to people and their businesses. That is why the buildings where banks keep their computer systems are often highly protected, with high fences outside, no windows, guards at the front door and complicated entry systems to let workers in and out.

The problem is, for many of these computer systems to work they must be allowed to talk to other computer systems. For instance, if someone buys a book over the **Internet,** their computer is talking to a computer that may well be sitting in a secure, carefully guarded building. The weakness is not in the real world, where you would not be allowed into the building even if you were buying a book from one of the computers inside. The weakness lies in the 'virtual', or 'cyber' world, a world made up of the Internet's phone lines and computer connections.

Cyber criminals do not attack buildings, they attack computers, and they get at the computers over the same links we use every day when we make telephone calls, send **email** or surf the **World Wide Web**.

5

What do cyber criminals do?

Theft and fraud

What are cyber criminals doing when they break into computer systems? The most obvious crime is stealing money. Cyber criminals have found ways to use other people's **credit cards** without their knowledge – without even having seen the card itself. They have also managed to persuade banks' computers to transfer money to them, and ordered goods and services without paying for them.

Other cyber criminals try to steal commercial secrets. These secrets might be taken for the thief's own use, or perhaps for someone else who is paying them. A big problem is when employees themselves turn into cyber criminals, and break into their own company's computer systems and damage important systems, or steal secrets. They might do this because of an argument, or a grudge against a co-worker or boss.

There are also people who, rather than break into computers themselves, design computer **viruses** that cause damage automatically. Virus creators are often computer programmers who want to show off their skills. They get satisfaction from outwitting makers of anti-virus software, which is designed to stop such crimes happening.

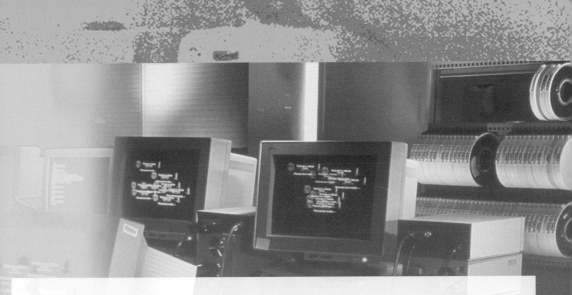

Racism and pornography

Another group of cyber criminals seeks to distribute illegal information. This may include racist material – for instance, there are websites that encourage people to attack or take other action against particular groups in society. Other sites might sell or pass on **pornography**. Police and child protection groups are particularly worried about sites featuring indecent pictures of children, and about other sites that allow children access to adult material.

There is also deep concern about information swapped between terrorists over the **Internet** – for example, detailed 'recipes' for making bombs. The problem for police forces around the world is that much of this material – from racist material to bomb recipes – is not illegal everywhere: countries around the world have different laws.

Sharing music

Perhaps the most widespread kind of cyber criminal is often the ordinary computer user. Swapping commercial music files – often known as **MP3s** – is very popular among some music lovers, but it is also a kind of theft, and is illegal in nearly every country in the world.

The spread of music-swapping services has been a big problem for the music industry, because many Internet users now listen to music that they have not paid for. This means that music companies, and the recording artists themselves, are having their work stolen. There have been court cases, mostly in the USA, aimed at closing down music-sharing services.

If you include all those who swap illegally copied MP3s, there are millions of cyber criminals around the world. It is just the seriousness of the crime that varies.

The first cyber criminals

Cyber crime might sound like a very new type of crime. In fact, it has been around since the early 1970s – before the **personal computer** was invented, when computers far less powerful than today's games consoles filled entire rooms and were looked after by technicians who wore white coats.

Phone 'phreaking'

The first cyber crimes were carried out across telephone lines, by a group of electronics enthusiasts known as 'phone phreakers'. They had studied the US telephone system, and realized it used a series of musical tones to connect calls. They found they could imitate those tones, and steal free phone calls, by creating small musical devices called 'blue boxes'. One famous 'phreaker', John Draper, even found that using a whistle given away inside a cereal box could do the same job as a blue box.

Draper became very serious about taking advantage of the weaknesses in the US telephone system. He drove around the US in a large van packed with equipment, taking it to remote spots where he would plug in to the telephone network and make illegal, free calls around the world.

Along the way, he was to prove an important influence to two young men, Steve Jobs and Steve Wozniak. They would later go on to found Apple

Steve Jobs, now Apple Computer chief executive, experimented with 'blue boxes' in his youth. He quickly moved on to use his computer skills in more legitimate ways.

Computer, one of the first personal computer companies, but in the early 1970s they were fascinated by 'phreaking', after seeing an article in a magazine, in which Draper explained his activities.

Jobs and Wozniak built a blue box to let them make free long-distance calls, just like Draper, but when they tried out their first blue box at a phone booth it did not go very well. The pair were caught by a passing police patrol and only escaped by telling the officers the device was a music synthesizer. Despite this close call, they met up with Draper and the three continued to experiment, once even making an illegal call from California to the Vatican City in Rome.

Going straight

However, in time, worried by the growing chance they would be caught, Jobs and Wozniak moved out of 'phreaking' and into computing, where they turned the technical skills they had developed building the blue boxes, to building computers – and made their fortunes. Draper was not so sensible – he was caught several times by police, found guilty of **defrauding** the telephone company, and jailed. He has now reformed, and runs a computer security company warning companies of the dangers of **hackers,** who try to break into computers.

The growth of cyber crime

For many years after Draper and Wozniak started making their blue boxes, cyber crime centered on the telephone, the aim being to get free or cheap telephone calls. The first computer-to-computer cyber crime did not happen until the 1980s.

The role of the Internet

It was the arrival of the **Internet** that was eventually to make cyber crime a big issue. The Internet linked together lots of small computer **networks**, into what is known as the **World Wide Web**. For the first time, computer users could 'talk' to each other direct.

The early cyber criminals were helped by ordinary computer users' lack of respect for the power of the Internet. For most people, cyber crime was not a worry. **Hackers** were thought to be harmless after being glamorized by the 1984 film *Wargames*, where a hacker saves the world.

The Internet was originally used by academics at universities, and by the military – and few people at these institutions were likely to want to damage the network. Because these were the people who developed the Internet, they took few precautions to make life harder for cyber criminals.

When millions of home and business computer users began to visit the Internet in the early to mid 1990s, few were thinking about the dangers of cyber crime, or about security. Banks and other big businesses were more interested in the benefits that computer networks could bring them, than in any possible dangers.

"This is not a tool we should take seriously, or our customers should take seriously."

(A Microsoft official telling the *New York Times* not to fear a new program that allows PCs to be hacked by cyber criminals, 1988)

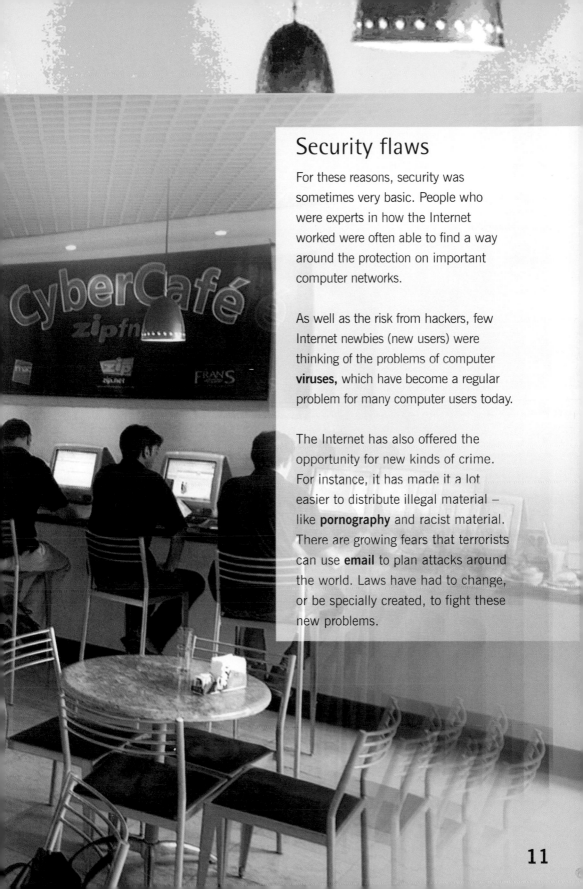

Security flaws

For these reasons, security was sometimes very basic. People who were experts in how the Internet worked were often able to find a way around the protection on important computer networks.

As well as the risk from hackers, few Internet newbies (new users) were thinking of the problems of computer **viruses,** which have become a regular problem for many computer users today.

The Internet has also offered the opportunity for new kinds of crime. For instance, it has made it a lot easier to distribute illegal material – like **pornography** and racist material. There are growing fears that terrorists can use **email** to plan attacks around the world. Laws have had to change, or be specially created, to fight these new problems.

The rise of the virus

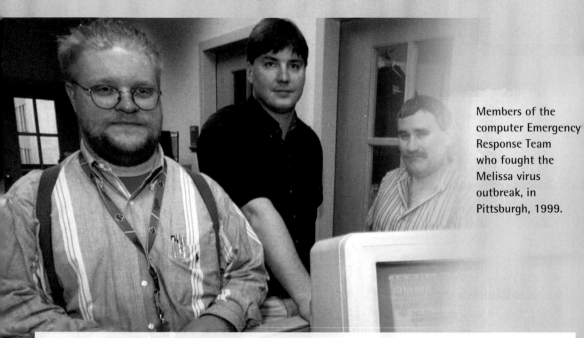

Members of the computer Emergency Response Team who fought the Melissa virus outbreak, in Pittsburgh, 1999.

When we fall ill, it is often because we have caught a bug, or **virus**, from someone else – perhaps a friend or member of our family. Computers get viruses too, and they pass from computer to computer very like a nasty human illness. One infected computer can pass on the bug, through the **Internet,** to many thousands of other computers.

What is a computer virus?

Computer viruses are small computer programs that arrive in someone's computer hidden in files on a diskette or attached to an **email.** Sometimes the virus is not designed to do anything, other than copy itself on to other users.

Other viruses are designed to pop a message on the screen on a particular date, although these viruses can accidentally cause other problems if they are not well programmed.

Increasingly, viruses are being created that are deliberately more damaging, wiping files and even entire disks, and carrying out **'denial of service'** (DOS) attacks on other machines on the Internet. DOS attacks are when computers around the Internet send lots of messages to a single target computer. The target cannot cope with all the messages, and stops working. Where many copies of a virus have started DOS attacks at the same time, some parts of the Internet have stopped working.

The Melissa virus

One of the earliest serious computer viruses was named 'Melissa' by its creators. It struck in March 1999, and targeted users of **software** made by the company Microsoft. The majority of computers use Microsoft software. When a user 'caught' the virus, an infected email would be sent secretly to the first 50 people on the user's email address book. It was not designed to cause problems, but the huge rise in the number of emails being sent – 50 from every infected user – meant that parts of the Internet quickly became jammed.

David Smith at a New Jersey courtroom.

David Smith, a 30-year-old programmer from New Jersey in the USA, was eventually arrested and charged with computer theft. He pleaded guilty to causing over $80 million in damage.

Since Melissa, many more viruses have been let loose. All these have been dealt with, although the costs have been high. Some people worry that one day a cyber criminal will deliberately create a virus that could halt the entire Internet. This could cause companies to lose massive sums of money, and cost people around the world their jobs.

Cyber crime overview

Fraud

Cyber crime started with **fraud**. The first person to be found guilty of cyber crime on a computer was 'Captain Zap' – real name Ian Murphy – in 1981, after he broke into a US telephone company computer and changed the internal clock so that customers were given cheap phone calls at peak times.

Hacking gained new public visibility after the 1984 film *Wargames*, in which a **hacker** breaks into a US military computer and saves the world. Many hackers later said this hit movie was their inspiration.

As hacking grew in popularity, phone companies were, often, still the victims. Kevin Mitnick was jailed in 1989 for breaking into a company computer system, and in 1993 three hackers were found guilty of hacking a telephone company so they could win a radio station phone-in competition. They 'won' $20,000 in cash, two sports cars and holidays in Hawaii before police caught up with them.

It seemed only a matter of time before banks became the new target; and in 1994 it happened. A group of Russian hackers broke into US bank Citibank's computers and stole $10 million. But the gang's ringleader was quickly caught, and all but $400,000 of their haul was recovered.

With the rise of the **Internet, credit cards** became tools of cyber criminals: Kevin Mitnick was (again) arrested for stealing 20,000 credit card numbers over the net in 1995. This and other credit card crime since has prompted credit card companies to consider ways they can make cards more secure.

Viruses

At first, **viruses** were spread by disks being passed between computers. The Michelangelo virus of 1991 was such a virus – it was programmed to wipe **hard drives** on the birthday of the famous Italian painter it was named after.

Now, viruses mainly spread over the Internet. There are many viruses around, but famous ones include 'Melissa', which cost $80 million in damage in 1999, and the 'ILOVEYOU' virus of 2000. In 1995, Briton Christopher Pile became the first person to be jailed for writing a virus.

Terrorism

Terrorism over the Internet is a new fear, following the terrorist attacks in New York and Washington in 2001, in which thousands of people died. After those attacks it was discovered the planners could have been communicating by **email.** In the USA, new laws were introduced to attempt to stop terrorists using coded email.

Who are the hackers?

Cyber criminals can cause great damage. Who on earth would want to become one?

There are several kinds of **hacker.** There are those who try to gain financially from their efforts. Some are company employees who bear a grudge against their boss, and set out to cause damage or leak secrets. And there is another group who are cracking computers for their own enjoyment, or to deliver a message about something they believe in. Even those who simply want to show off can cause great damage.

The case of Raphael Gray

Nineteen-year-old Raphael Gray was a computer enthusiast from a small town in Wales. Gray read about a weakness in some computer **software** used by several **online** stores, which meant that it would be possible for him to get details of **credit cards** customers had used on the sites. He could then use the card details to go shopping.

Gray used the weakness to break into the online stores, and stole the details of 25,000 credit cards. Instead of keeping them to himself, he then posted the details of 6000 cards to a website. Anyone who looked at that website could have used the card details. Gray also used the card of a customer called Bill Gates to send prescription drugs to the famous Bill Gates, chairman of Microsoft, as a joke.

The credit card companies found out about Gray's **scam**, however, and spent £2 million refunding customers whose cards were misused, and issuing replacement cards to all the customers affected.

Hacker Onel de Guzman, suspect in the 'ILOVEYOU' **virus** case. This virus stole computer users' passwords and emailed them to others, affecting thousands of people around the world.

The FBI was also alerted to Gray's activities and he was quickly caught – despite his boasting on Internet **chatboards** that he was a skilled hacker, they had found it easy to trace his address. Early one morning the police raided his home, where he lived with his parents, and Gray was arrested. He pleaded guilty to breaking into computer systems in the UK, the USA and Canada and to 'obtaining services by deception', and was sentenced to three years' community rehabilitation, with an order to seek psychiatric help.

Gray did not make any personal gain from his crimes, but the cost to others – credit card companies and online stores – of his crime was huge. The card users were also affected, with a great deal of worry and wasted time. A spokesman for one of the credit card firms affected by Gray's crimes summed it up. 'This is not a victimless crime,' he said.

A technical expert with the Philippines National Bureau of Investigation displays a computer disk seized from the apartment of Onel de Guzman.

17

Friend or foe?

Raphael Gray, like other cyber criminals, cost businesses millions of pounds, and caused thousands of **credit card** users problems, with his cyber attacks. Gray says he did not set out to do this: his plan, he claimed, was to draw attention to security holes in popular **software,** to stop other cyber criminals from carrying out more serious crimes.

Many cyber criminals say this when caught, or when they talk about their actions. They say that what they are doing is not for their own gain, but to improve security and embarrass software makers. There is fierce debate between people who say what these 'friendly **hackers**' do can be justified, and those who say all such behaviour is wrong.

For instance, one 'friendly hacker' in the USA has discovered several major security flaws at big companies. The twenty-year-old will break into computer systems and then tell the company about what he has done, so they can fix the hole he discovered. He does not attempt to steal from the companies he breaks into, or encourage others to do so, but he is still breaking the law. The only time hacking can be legal is when companies – keen to find weak spots in their computer security – pay skilled hackers to try and break into their systems. Some former hackers, like John Draper, now turn their expertise to helping big companies keep the hackers out.

Some say people commit cyber crime not for the money, but for the recognition they gain. Cyber crime has been made to look glamorous by films and big-name hackers, and not as serious as crimes in the 'real' world. There is also a strong community of hackers, who boast to each other about their exploits and swap tips. Some even create software to make hacking into other computers easy. All these things can make cyber crime seem less serious than it is.

A teenage hacker, known as 'Coolio', after being sentenced to nine months in jail in New Hampshire, USA. He pleaded guilty to hacking into national computer sites belonging to the Army and the Air Force.

Kevin Mitnick

The most notorious hacker in the world is Kevin Mitnick. He started his criminal career aged just seventeen, and is seen as a hero by some would-be cyber criminals. In 1989 he was convicted of stealing software and codes for long-distance telephone lines, and was sent to prison for a year. Five years later, after using his skills to create several fake new identities and staying on the run for two years, he was caught again. He was charged with several crimes, including stealing 20,000 **credit card** numbers and secret plans from several companies. This time his sentence included five years in prison, including eight months in solitary confinement, and a long ban on using computers.

"I am not innocent but I certainly didn't do most of what I was accused of. A hacker doesn't deliberately destroy data or profit from his activities. I never made any money directly from hacking. I wasn't malicious."

Kevin Mitnick on his release from jail in 2000.

(Kevin Mitnick, quoted in *Wired News*, October 2001)

Creating havoc:
the organized groups

Not all organized groups of cyber criminals are breaking the law to make money. Like some **hackers** who work alone, some groups just want to see if they can cause chaos.

One hackers' group has released computer programs that make it possible to control other people's **PCs** across the **Internet**, without the computers' owners being aware that their computers are being accessed. Despite the fact that the program allows hackers to break the law by using another person's computer without permission, it is a matter of pride for its makers that they have managed to exploit this security hole.

Other groups have created programs and websites that make it possible to create a working **credit card** number. This number might be one that belongs to someone already, or it might be one that has not yet been allocated. Such programs and websites, again, encourage others to break the law by making cyber crime easier.

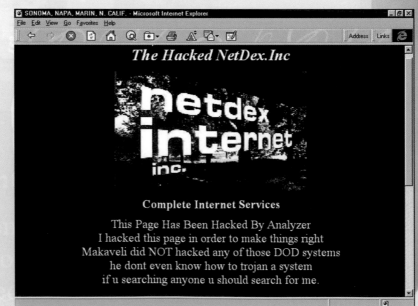

A page from a website after hacking by the Israeli hacker 'Analyzer'.

SONOMA, NAPA, MARIN, N. CALIF. - Microsoft Internet Explorer

File Edit View Go Favorites Help

Address Links

The Hacked NetDex.Inc

netdex internet inc.

Complete Internet Services

This Page Has Been Hacked By Analyzer
I hacked this page in order to make things right
Makaveli did NOT hacked any of those DOD systems
he dont even know how to trojan a system
if u searching anyone u should search for me.

Why do some people want to encourage cyber crime?

The creators of such **software** would argue that, by doing so, they are exposing the poor security of popular software, or credit cards. Like the 'friendly hackers' discussed earlier, these groups say they are performing a service.

This may sometimes be true and, certainly, a number of security holes have been closed as software companies like Microsoft, and the credit card companies, work to make their security better. It can also be argued that the hacker groups have other, less honourable motives. When they expose another 'exploit', as they call the security holes they find, they get the credit for the discovery. Getting the admiration and praise of friends and colleagues is important, and perhaps especially for members of hacker groups where the only way the members really know each other is through their 'exploits'.

Israeli master-hacker Ehud Tenebaum, aged eighteen, code-named 'Analyzer', after eleven hours of police questioning over a cyber assault on the Pentagon's computer systems.

The superhighway robbers

Imagine a cyber criminal and you might think of a nerdy young man, sitting in a dark room, communicating with nobody and nothing – apart from his computer. It is certainly easier to imagine individuals wanting to create chaos on the **Internet** than entire groups.

Even so, just as with crime in the 'real' world, some of the biggest cyber crimes have been pulled off by groups of people, working together and combining their abilities to reach their goal. That goal might be to encourage widespread hacking, steal a lot of money, or spread chaos through a **virus.**

The Citibank robbery

For instance, in 1994, a Russian gang carried out the first ever publicly revealed '**network** robbery' of a bank. Young **hacker**, Vladimir Levin, used his skills to access Citibank's computer network and steal a list of customer codes and passwords. He then logged in to the network eighteen times over several weeks, and moved $3.7 million from victims' bank accounts to other accounts around the world, operated by the gang.

The crime was noticed when customers realized money was disappearing from their accounts, and complained to the bank. The international police force, Interpol, managed to trace Levin to London, and he was eventually jailed for three years. Four members of the gang admitted conspiracy to commit bank **fraud,** and were also punished.

There were several worrying things about this crime. First, banks realized they were now targets for a new breed of criminal, the cyber criminal. They would have to tighten up their security in order to look after their customers.

Second, Levin was not a loner working by himself. He was part of a gang that had carefully masterminded the crime. Had they succeeded, it would have been one of the biggest bank robberies in history – without a single shot being fired or safe being dynamited.

The nature of the Internet, and the number of people connected to it, means that crimes carried out by cyber criminals could claim more victims than ever before. For most people, the chances of being robbed in the street are very low. If cyber crime were allowed to grow, the chances of being affected by crime – 'cyber' rather than 'real life' – could suddenly become much higher.

Credit card crime explained

When we hear about cyber criminals breaking into websites, we often hear they are doing it to steal **credit card** details. Why?

The first reason is that every **online** shop holds lots of credit card details in its computers. Nine out of every ten purchases over the **Internet** involve a credit card. Without credit cards, we would have to use other methods that would not be nearly as convenient – like posting a cheque, or transferring cash from one bank to another. Credit cards make online shopping very fast and easy but, because of this, the computers that hold all a website's customer details are also the cyber criminals' first targets.

The second problem is the way credit cards work. Because credit cards were designed many years ago, long before the Internet, they are easy for cyber criminals to defraud. Once a cyber criminal has a stolen credit card number, it is possible for him or her to buy things online straight away.

How do credit cards work?

Credit cards allow people over eighteen to pay for things without needing to carry lots of cash.

The customer is given a plastic credit card by a card issuer like MasterCard or Visa. These companies have agreements with shops around the world, which each pay a small fee for every payment they take using the card.

Each credit card carries a unique number and the customer's signature on the back. When the customer wants to buy something using a card, the shop copies the card, including the unique number, and asks the customer to sign a slip of paper. The signature on the slip of paper is checked against the signature on the back of the card – if they match, the shop knows the person making the purchase is also the card owner.

Credit cards were designed long before the **World Wide Web** existed and, over the Internet, signatures cannot be matched. This means that all a cyber criminal needs in order to buy something online is a stolen credit card with a name, number and the date on which the card runs out.

This means credit card companies are now looking at other ways to check the shopper is also the cardholder, which might help stop credit card cyber crime. These include individual pin-numbers to be entered with other details, putting special microchips in the cards, and only sending goods to the billing address, rather than to a separate delivery address.

A victimless crime?

This book has already looked at some of the damage cyber crime does. But how does this affect ordinary people? After all, the banks are the ones losing all the money when cyber criminals attack. Big companies have to pick up the bill if **viruses** bring down the **Internet. Credit card** companies even protect their customers, which means the cardholder does not have to pay the cost of any **fraud**.

All this is true, but it is still ordinary people – as citizens, shoppers and computer users – who eventually pay the price for cyber crime. How? The problem lies in the way victims of crime – computer users, shops and other businesses – recover after criminals have struck.

Spreading the cost

For example, many people buy insurance – that is, they make a regular payment to an insurance company to protect their belongings. Then, if they lose something through theft or accident, the insurance company pays for the stolen or damaged goods to be replaced. The insurance company makes money because many more people buy insurance than are the victims of crime or accidents.

However, if more people become victims of cyber crime, the insurance companies will have to pay out more money – and that means they will have to charge all their customers more in order to pay the increased number of claims. Because insurance companies often insure a range of things – from bicycles to whole warehouses – the monthly amount for everything is likely to go up. If there was a wave of cyber crime, even someone who had never used the Internet could end up helping to pay for it.

The same problem exists in other areas too: take the example of credit cards. If a cyber criminal uses a credit card, the card company will make sure the card's real owner does not have to pay the bill. In the past, the credit card company would meet the cost itself, paid for by the money it charges its customers to borrow, or through fees charged to shops.

However, once the card companies realized the bill for cyber crime could be huge, they changed the rules. Today the same card companies do not pick up the bill for crime themselves – but pass it back to the online stores. In order to make sure they have some money spare to pay the bill for credit card fraud, shops have to raise their prices, so we all end up paying for cyber crime.

Many **online** shops do not exist only in the online world. The biggest names in our shopping malls and high streets often have big websites, and that creates another problem: what happens if a major high street store is hit by cyber crime? Imagine if a major chain store's website was closed down by cyber criminals. It would mean the huge warehouses where stock is held would be lying unused. Whole buildings full of customer services representatives would be silent, and delivery vans would be standing still.

The cost to the whole business – not just the **Internet** part – would be huge, because all these people and all these buildings would still have to be paid for, whether they were working or not. When businesses are faced with big losses, they often have to cut jobs. People are made unemployed, shareholders in the company see their dividends (share of profits) fall, and the service to us all gets poorer.

The knock-on effect

The side effects of cyber crime live on long after the major problem created by the criminals themselves has been cured. Today, many people are still worried about buying things over the Internet, because they fear their **credit card** details may be misused. When people see in newspapers or on TV that a big fraud has taken place, two things may happen. First, their confidence in online shopping is shaken, and they are less likely to use the Internet to shop. Second, if a particular online store has been the victim of cyber criminals, shoppers are likely to avoid using it. The overall effects of this are that online stores are less likely to make a profit, and that customers may be denied many of the good things about online shopping – a wide choice, the chance of bargains and the ease of shopping. It can also spell disaster for the online business – lost profits, more jobs cut, even the closure of services we all find useful. Even if cyber criminals do not directly touch us, they can still reach out and affect our lives.

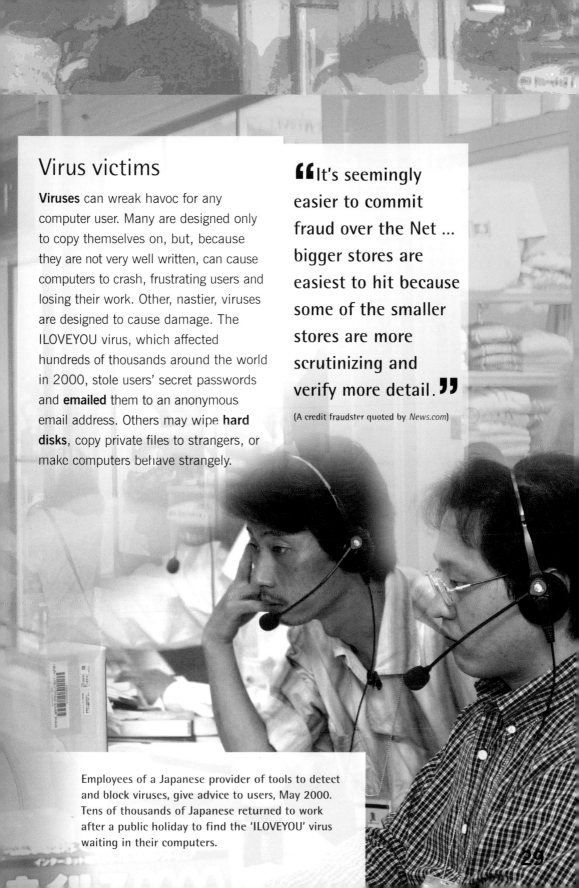

Virus victims

Viruses can wreak havoc for any computer user. Many are designed only to copy themselves on, but, because they are not very well written, can cause computers to crash, frustrating users and losing their work. Other, nastier, viruses are designed to cause damage. The ILOVEYOU virus, which affected hundreds of thousands around the world in 2000, stole users' secret passwords and **emailed** them to an anonymous email address. Others may wipe **hard disks**, copy private files to strangers, or make computers behave strangely.

❝It's seemingly easier to commit fraud over the Net ... bigger stores are easiest to hit because some of the smaller stores are more scrutinizing and verify more detail.**❞**

(A credit fraudster quoted by *News.com*)

Employees of a Japanese provider of tools to detect and block viruses, give advice to users, May 2000. Tens of thousands of Japanese returned to work after a public holiday to find the 'ILOVEYOU' virus waiting in their computers.

29

Credit card fraud victims

There have been many victims of **credit card fraud**, but the worst-hit group is **online** shops. Credit cards were designed to be used face to face. Online stores, though, operate in a 'virtual' world, where they cannot see the person making the purchase. That means they are much easier targets for cyber criminals.

Online companies

It is difficult to get exact details of how many online shops have been damaged by cyber crime, because some do not want to admit they have been hit for fear of driving away customers. But surveys show that only half of all businesses see the **Internet** as a safe place to buy and sell goods and services. Around seven in every ten businesses have been recent victims of cyber crime.

Some companies even say cyber crime has helped force them out of business. Flooz.com, a US **website** endorsed by Hollywood actress Whoopi Goldberg, went out of business in 2001. Flooz.com was an online gift certificate site where users could buy 'Flooz points' to give as presents to friends and family. The points could be spent at various online shops.

Just months before Flooz went out of business, police were called in when it was alleged a ring of cyber criminals from Eastern Europe had used stolen credit card details to buy Flooz points. Banks stopped all payments for goods bought using Flooz points, and a million dollars of the company's money was held, in case there was a big bill from stolen Flooz points. In the end, the company had to pay $300,000 on top of that for goods bought using the stolen Flooz points.

With a big chunk of its money frozen, but customers continuing to spend their Flooz points, the company closed its website in August 2001, saying credit card fraud had played a part in its problems. Many users were upset that they could no longer use the Flooz points they had saved up or even paid for.

Cyber criminals have almost forced other **e-commerce** sites out of business in this way, and there is now great pressure on the credit card companies to think up ways to solve the problem.

Individual victims

For the ordinary person, credit card fraud is a real problem, too. The first they might know of a crime is when their bill shows purchases they have not made. Then they have to call their credit card company and try to prove they did not buy these things. An investigation is launched, and a new card must be issued. In the end, a victim should not have to pay directly for the fraud, but will suffer a great deal of inconvenience and worry. There are fears that if this type of fraud is not stopped, people will be reluctant to use their credit cards on the Internet.

The launch of the Internet Fraud Complaint Center, set up in Washington D.C., USA, to tackle the growing problem of Internet fraud.

Software: functions versus flaws

Some cyber criminals target the **software** used on computers. Modern programs often include lots of time-saving features designed to make users' lives easier. For instance, functions called '**macros**' can carry out boring or repetitive tasks, while **email** address books mean users don't have to memorize the address of every person they know.

Worms

Cyber criminals have come up with a special kind of **virus,** called a worm, to attack these pieces of software. Like a real earthworm, this program can duplicate itself. It sends copies of itself over a network, and then the copies send copies of themselves – and so on.

This kind of virus creates a big problem for **Internet** users. A worm will often use the macro function built into popular software to copy itself to everyone in a user's address book. If they have stored a lot of addresses, that means an awful lot of email is going to be sent out very quickly without their permission. If lots of computers do this all at the same time, it can over-burden the Internet, causing it to work more slowly or even break down.

"In some ways, I'm surprised that they haven't brought down the Internet."

(Robert Graham of computer security firm, Network ICE, talking to News.com about Internet worms)

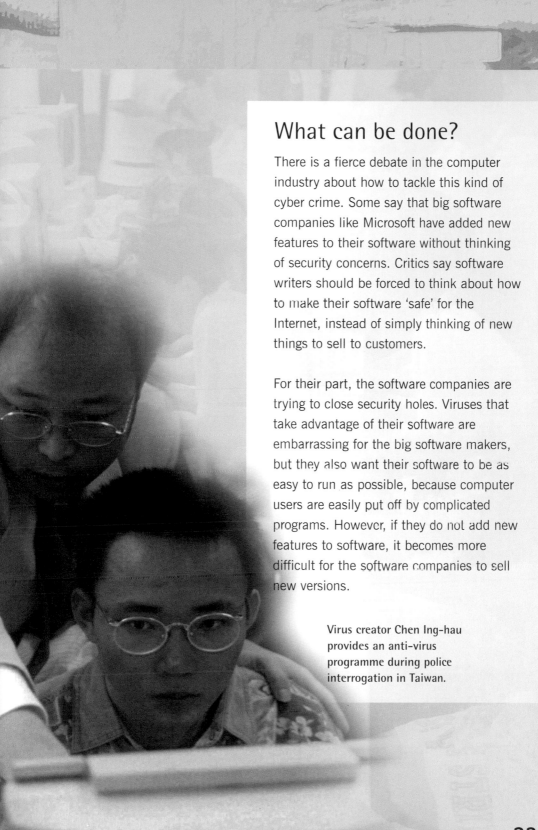

What can be done?

There is a fierce debate in the computer industry about how to tackle this kind of cyber crime. Some say that big software companies like Microsoft have added new features to their software without thinking of security concerns. Critics say software writers should be forced to think about how to make their software 'safe' for the Internet, instead of simply thinking of new things to sell to customers.

For their part, the software companies are trying to close security holes. Viruses that take advantage of their software are embarrassing for the big software makers, but they also want their software to be as easy to run as possible, because computer users are easily put off by complicated programs. However, if they do not add new features to software, it becomes more difficult for the software companies to sell new versions.

Virus creator Chen Ing-hau provides an anti-virus programme during police interrogation in Taiwan.

Music on the Internet

One big area of discussion surrounds **online** music and video. For some time, it has been possible to get free copies of pieces of music or films through online services that allow computer users to swap files.

The first of these services was called Napster. At its peak it allowed millions of people to swap **MP3** files – files that contained all kinds of music – for free. One person could buy an album, use a computer to make an MP3 file of it and swap this file for another he or she hadn't bought. In this way, the person paid for one album but used it to get two. They didn't have to spend much money to have the latest chart hits.

What people were doing on Napster was actually illegal: by making MP3 files and sharing them with anyone, they were '**pirating**' music, which meant that the recording artists and their record companies were not being paid for their work. This version of Napster was eventually shut down after a series of court cases in the USA, although the Napster name lives on through a legal, paid-for music service.

However, there are still ways for **Internet** users to share their music collections, and record companies have

experimented with ways to stop them. Not all the record company's methods have been popular.

For instance, one of their first ideas was to make CDs that could only be played on normal CD players, and not on the CD players in computers, so computer users would no longer be able to make MP3 copies of the CDs. But this was unpopular with many people, who complained that their right to play music through their computers was being denied. Some also argued that copyright laws allowed them to make a single copy of a CD they had bought, if it was only for their own use.

Other ways to cut down on pirating of music have included making it more difficult to copy computer music files by using special encoding. But users say this makes it harder for them to enjoy the music on different devices, like portable music players.

Striking a balance

A debate continues between music companies and their customers. Record labels want to safeguard their businesses – if people expect music for nothing, the record companies will not have enough money to pay today's stars or find the stars of tomorrow. On the other hand, it might be harmful for record labels to upset their customers too much by clamping down on copying, and it might even encourage people to break the law.

The Napster website displays a newsflash about its music-sharing services.

The law versus freedom

Cyber crime comes in many different forms and causes great damage to **Internet** users and Internet businesses. Yet the law struggles to deal with cyber crimes and the people who commit them.

Why are there not stronger laws? There are several problems for the politicians who have to make decisions about rules and laws.

Sergeant Mark Lauer searches confiscated computers in Vermont. Police are now having to deal with computer crime including child pornography, business **fraud** and **email harassment**.

Free speech

The first problem is the right to free speech. Free speech – the right to hold an opinion and tell others about it – is a central part of any democracy, a basic human right. In some countries – the USA, for instance – the right to free speech is written down in the **constitution**. If free speech is seen as a basic right, then any law that might restrict free speech has to be very carefully thought out, as the law itself could be illegal. For instance, in the late 1990s there were plans in the USA to restrict the kind of material – in particular **pornography** – that could be placed on the Internet.

Campaigners managed to stop this, because they argued such laws would have restricted freedom of expression. They argued that if a law were introduced to restrict one kind of Internet material, it would be much easier from then on to introduce laws to shut down other kinds of website. Websites, they argued, should not be closed or censored just because some people disagree with what they show.

International boundaries

The second difficulty in creating new laws for the Internet is that the Internet goes across international borders, while most laws do not. In some countries, laws on Internet use are more relaxed. This might be because the Internet is not popular enough yet in a particular country for it to have created new laws, or it might be that such laws are not seen as a priority. This has a big effect on the Internet as a whole. Criminals can log on to the Internet from a country with slack cyber crime laws, and attack computers many thousands of miles away without fear of punishment.

There are plans to create more international laws to fight cyber crime. However, such agreements – called **treaties** – take time to organize and discuss.

Detective Sergeant
Tim Lee, of the CID
Computer Crimes
Unit, Michigan, USA.

The rise of the security industry

What can be done to stop cyber criminals? Just as in the real world, where we fit better locks and sturdier doors to keep out intruders, so the **Internet** world has tried to improve its security. In fact, a whole new industry has been created to help make the Internet a safer place.

First of all, individual users have been encouraged to take more responsibility for their **online** safety. Most of us would not leave our front doors unlocked, yet many people have, until recently, put their computers on the Internet without any thought about security.

Now more computer users know about the dangers of **viruses,** more people are installing special virus-checking **software** to protect against what might arrive in their **email.** This software filters everything the computer receives, and can remove any viruses it recognizes.

❝There are fourteen-year-old kids out there who can do things well beyond what someone with a computer science degree would dream of.❞

(John Klein, from the company Rent-A-Hacker)

Firewall protection

Computer users are also being encouraged to install special '**firewall**' software. A firewall is a computer program that works a bit like a bouncer at a nightclub. Every bit of information coming into the computer from the Internet is checked. If not suspicious, it is allowed through. Anything that looks dangerous is blocked, and the user is alerted.

Typed 'conversation' between hackers, intercepted by the Honeynet Project.

Lance Spitzner, founder of the Honeynet Project.

The Honeynet Project has become one of the leading efforts to monitor the hacker community. A 30-strong team receives phone messages when computer networks under observation are being attacked.

Changing sides

Helping this new industry are many former **hackers,** who have now decided to use their computer skills to protect others. The help from these reformed cyber criminals is often particularly valuable. Not only are they skilled computer users, but they also understand how hackers think. By asking themselves 'What would I do in this situation?' they can often close a security hole before it is found in public.

Even the most famous of phone 'phreakers' – John Draper, who was also known as Captain Crunch – now runs his own company, called Webcrunchers, which offers help with computer security. Businesses are particularly keen to get specialist help and advice on security. It often comes as a surprise to employers that one of the most common problems they might face is when staff turn against them, and seek to damage computer systems.

❝Once a virus is out there it can't be reclaimed, so we wouldn't hire a former virus writer, because the damage from a virus is never-ending.❞

(Jimmy Kuo, of anti-virus company McAfee)

39

Selling security

Cyber crime has hit **online** stores particularly hard. Their challenge has been to make sure that customers' details are safe from the prying eyes of **hackers** – and also to reassure customers that they really are safe.

As already discussed, many people have read about **credit card fraud** in newspapers, or seen stories about it on TV, so it has been difficult to persuade them that their details will be safe when shopping. Around the world, surveys show that it takes a long time for **Internet** users to become confident in using their credit cards to buy things online.

Staying safe

The best stores, therefore, go to great lengths to prove they are safe to use. For instance, Amazon.com – the biggest online shop there is – points out on its website that tens of millions of customers have shopped with them without credit card fraud taking place.

At several points on their website, Amazon.com reminds customers that it uses Secure Sockets Layer (SSL) technology – an accepted way of **encrypting** (scrambling) messages between computers. And, should fraud

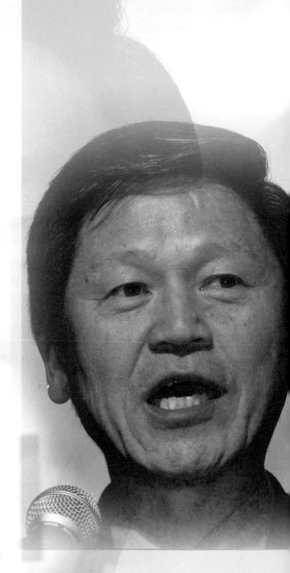

ever happen on its site, Amazon tells customers their credit card companies protect them for all but the first $50 lost. Amazon will even pay that for any **defrauded** customer not covered. For those customers still too worried to give their credit card details online, Amazon offers a service that allows you to complete your purchase over the telephone.

Many other **e-commerce** sites now do the same, and some even use trusted organizations – like consumer associations – to confirm independently that they have taken proper precautions.

All this activity ensures that security is tight between the shopper and the online store, and also does the important job of helping customers feel comfortable sharing their credit card details over the **World Wide Web**.

Finally, credit card companies are exploring new ways to make their cards more secure. For instance, some card issuers are already offering 'one use' card numbers, which can only be used to buy things once. The challenge for everybody concerned – shops, computer users and card companies – is to stay one step ahead of the cyber criminals.

New initiatives: the launch of a credit card loaded with a computer chip to make Internet shopping easier and more secure.

Fighting cyber crime

It is clearly a good idea to make it difficult to carry out cyber crime. Sometimes, though, even the tightest security is not enough, which is why great effort is being made to find new ways to catch cyber criminals.

One of the first lessons police forces learned was that, when it comes to cyber crime, national borders no longer matter. It is just as easy (or difficult) for a criminal based in Moscow to raid an American bank over the **Internet** as it is for a **hacker** in New York.

International co-operation

What does this mean? It means that police forces from different countries have to work much more closely together to fight cyber crime. This is not easy – not least because each country has different laws, and what is illegal in one country might be allowed in another.

But on several important issues, including fraud and some kinds of illegal content – such as **pornography** and illegally copied **software** – most countries in the world agree. The case of Vladimir Levin and the Russian gang who robbed Citibank in 1994 was solved by police forces around the world working together. The international police organization, Interpol, helped co-ordinate police action during the Citibank case. Now Interpol has working parties on cyber crime across the world. They bring experts from different countries together to offer advice and practical help to each other.

There are also attempts to create an international **treaty** on cyber crime – a set of laws that would apply to most of the Internet-using countries in the world. International treaties, however, take time to discuss because of the large number of countries involved. There is a great deal of opposition to the idea of such a treaty: some people say these new laws would harm civil rights, and destroy some of the best things about the Internet.

One outcome of the possible new rules is that it could become much more difficult to do things on the Internet without revealing exactly who you are. This would help cut down on **fraud,** but it would also make it difficult for important services like **online** support groups to exist. These can carry out important functions: for instance, allowing teenagers to talk honestly about problems at home or school with counsellors, without fear of being identified – and without fear that friends, teachers or parents will find out.

A hacker known as 'Mudge' testifies before
a US Senate Committee. He told the committee
that computer security is so lax, hackers could
disable the entire Internet in a half-hour.

Media focus

'Cyber zombies' sound more like something out of a bad film than something that could actually exist and cause harm in the real word. Yet one newspaper in Australia, the *Sun Herald*, warned of an attack of the 'cyber zombies' in October 2000, telling its readers: 'Don't laugh – this is billion-dollar serious.' Cyber zombies were meant to be **viruses** that could infect a computer and sit waiting for a certain date or event to trigger them. However, cyber zombies have yet to show up.

Meanwhile an alert, issued by the FBI, about a new **Internet** worm called 'Code Red', made headlines on television networks around the world, including the USA's CNN and Britain's BBC. It was feared the virus would bring down the Internet only hours later but, in fact, it failed to have much effect at all.

These are just two examples of the massive amount of coverage given to cyber crime since the Internet became popular, and both show how newspapers and television can sometimes make potential problems seem far worse than they actually are.

Both these stories caused a great deal of concern. With any virus scare, businesses spend time and money checking their systems. Scares, even if later proved to be exaggerated, create fears that the Internet is not a safe place to spend time or do business.

EXPERT WARNS OF ATTACK OF THE CYBER 'ZOMBIES'

By John Hampshire, Technology Writer

A global expert on cybercrime, Chris Rouland, warns that thousands of Australian computers have been infected with zombies ready to launch attacks that will cripple commercial sites such as Amazon.com, costing operators millions of dollars. His warning comes as new data shows fraud costs Australia more than $3 billion a year.

Beware, Australia, the zombies are out to get you. But don't laugh, because this is billion-dollar serious. Zombies are programs that lie dormant until they're told to cripple computers with huge amounts of bogus data.

The e-crime report released by the Australasian Centre for Policing Research also says latest estimates are that $960 billion in illicit cash is laundered globally each year. Hacker and fraud attacks are swamping authorities.

Source: *Sun Herald*, Australia 29 October 2000.

Getting things in perspective

There are several reasons why this happens. First, cyber crime is a very new area. Not everyone knows a great deal about computers, or how the Internet works, so sometimes people get confused and worry about things that are not as serious as they fear.

For instance, there has actually been very little crime committed against people who are buying things using a secure **web server** – most crimes happen when **credit cards**, or the numbers on them, are stolen from somewhere else.

Second, a great deal of hype (over-the-top publicity) surrounds Internet security. There is no shortage of 'experts' – many of whom are interested in selling Internet security products – willing to tell a TV camera or newspaper reporter that there are 'cyber zombies' or 'killer net worms' on the loose. In films and TV dramas, **hackers** are portrayed as powerful, clever criminals who can crack any system, when in reality this is unlikely.

Of course, as more people get used to the Internet, and realize what the real dangers are, media coverage will also improve, and reflect what is going on in the **online** world. And that may have one positive side effect: with some of the misplaced glamour and mystery removed from cyber crime, fewer people might be tempted to break the law.

Still from the film Wargames, about a hacker who saves the world.

How not to be a cyber criminal

One of the problems with the **Internet** is that it makes breaking the law very easy. For instance, downloading illegal copies of music – like **MP3** files – from the net is perhaps the easiest way to become a cyber criminal.

There are many places **online** where people can pick up the latest chart hits for nothing, although record companies are now working to get laws passed which could close down these services, and to have those responsible punished with heavy fines.

They are doing this because record companies rely on music sales to pay bands and singers. If that money is not coming in, record companies cannot spend as much searching for new talent, making it even harder for good new bands to get a record deal. You can avoid making the situation worse by using the official, paid-for music sites on the net, or downloading from sites that offer free samples of up-and-coming bands.

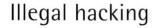

Illegal hacking

Another easy way to break the law is to try **hacking** computer systems. Some people do not realize that even attempting to get into a computer or Internet account by guessing the password is cyber crime, but in many countries it is just as illegal as the kind of hacking carried out by professional hackers like Kevin Mitnick. You are unlikely to go to jail for guessing a password, but breaking into an account could get you disconnected from the Internet, not to mention cause you embarrassment. Your school, or your Internet provider, will have rules on what users can – and cannot – do.

Finally, be careful about what you download and pass on over the Internet. Files you might think funny or interesting may be seen by others as annoying or offensive. The safest thing to do is check the rules – and laws – on what you can look at on the Internet, and what you can keep stored on your machine. If you are in any doubt about material, it is safer not to download it, and certainly not to pass it on.

Internet safety checklist

On your computer

- Make sure your computer is secure with up-to-date **virus** protection. You can find virus checker programs free **online** or buy one at a computer store. Follow the maker's instructions for keeping the virus checker up to date.

- If you use a shared computer at school or in a cybercafe, do not use the 'remember password' option that is available on some websites – other people will be able to get in and pretend they are you!

- When using shared computers, always close any open **browser** windows and log off after you have finished.

- Make it hard for the **hacker**. If you have a cable or other 'always on' **Internet** connection (one where you don't dial up) it is a very good idea to install a **firewall** program. This is a kind of locked front door for your computer. Again, you can get these free online or buy one at your local computer store.

- Do not use someone else's login, even if you think they would not mind.

On the Internet

- Be careful in **chatrooms**: people may not be who they say they are.

- Never arrange to meet someone you have met over the Internet.

- Never give out personal information like your address or phone number.

- Think twice about 'sharing' **MP3** music collections with other people, or downloading music from unofficial Internet services. If you share or download copyright music, you could be breaking the law.

- Remember, it is your responsibility to know what you are allowed to look at on the Internet. Never be tempted to break the rules, as it is easy to get caught out.

Online shopping

- Make sure you know how long it will take for delivery, and exactly what everything is going to cost, before buying. Is there a postal address for the company you are buying from? This means you can contact them if you have a complaint.

- Make sure the online shop you want to use has secure ordering. Most browser programs will indicate that you are using an **encrypted** connection with a symbol such as a key or padlock, in one of the status bars.

- Always print out the confirmation screen after you have ordered, as proof of your order.

- Be very wary of online auctions, and only buy from people with recommendations from other users.

Email

- Do not open email attachments unless you are sure what is in them, even if they come from someone you know.

- Only send attachments when it is really necessary – put your message in a plain note instead.

- Take no notice of email warning you of virus threats, especially those that urge you to send the warning to your friends. These warnings are nearly always hoaxes. If you are worried, check out the database of hoaxes and real threats at your anti-virus software maker's website.

- Never send abusive email; never send email when you are angry.

Facts and figures

The threat within

In June 2001, 57 per cent of companies told research company Digital Research that their worst security breaches happened when their own users accessed information they were not supposed to see.

According to Information Security magazine, **viruses** hit 88 per cent of US companies in 2001 – despite 90 per cent of companies having virus protection in place.

The fear factor

In a poll for The Information Technology Association of America and Tumbleweed Communications Corp (December 2001):

- 71 per cent of respondents said they were 'very' or 'somewhat' concerned about **Internet** and computer security.

- 78 per cent of respondents said they were either 'very' or 'somewhat' concerned that personal information held by the government could be misused.

- 74 per cent expressed worries about terrorists using the Internet to launch cyber attacks against critical infrastructure – 37 per cent said they were 'very' concerned, while another 37 per cent said they were 'somewhat' concerned.

The growth of Internet crime

CERT defines an incident as an attempt (successful or not) to gain unauthorized access to a system or its data; and also a disruption or denial of service. One incident might involve a single computer, or thousands. The number of worldwide Internet security 'incidents' reported each year:

1991	1992	1993	1994	1995	1996	1997	1998	1999	2000	2001
406	773	1,334	2,340	2,412	2,573	2,134	3,734	9,859	21,756	34,754

Source: CERT (http://www.cert.org/stats/cert_stats.html)

Computer security costs the Australian department of defense $8 million (Australian dollars) a year. $1 million of that was for a special team of '**hacker** busters' to prevent cyber attacks.

Further information

General advice

CERT

US government organization that tracks **Internet** security incidents.
email: cert@cert.org
www.cert.org

National Consumer League

1701 K Street,
N.W., Suite 1200,
Washington D.C. 20006
Tel: (202) 835 3323
email: info@nclnet.org
www.nclnet.org/shoppingonline/

The National Consumer League is a US organization, but its advice on safe shopping **online** will be of use to Internet users around the world.

SANS

Professional institute that publishes tutorials and runs training courses on security.
www.sans.org

Symantec

Security firm Symantec runs a useful virus encyclopedia.
http://securityresponse.symantec.com/ avcenter/vinfodb.html

Contacts in the UK

The Internet Watch Foundation

5 Coles Lane, Oakington,
Cambridgeshire, CB4 5BA
Hotline: 01223 237700
email: admin@iwf.org.uk
www.iwf.org.uk/

The Internet Watch Foundation was set up by UK Internet service providers to help deal with the problem of illegal material on the Internet. You can report illegal material to the foundation, which will then seek to have it removed. Their website also offers useful safe surfing tips.

Which? Online

Castlemead, Gascoyne Way
Hertford X, SG14 1YB
Tel: 01992 822888
email: webtrader@which.net
http://whichwebtrader.which.net/

The Which? webtrader scheme vets **e-commerce** sites and awards safe ones its webtrader seal, which is then displayed on its website.

Contacts in the USA

The Consumer Federation of America

1424 16th St, NW, Suite 604,
Washington, D.C. 20036

The Consumer Federation of America takes a particular interest in the safety of children on the Internet, and users' privacy as they use Internet services.

The National Infrastructure Protection Center
J. Edgar Hoover Building,
935 Pennsylvania Avenue,
NW Washington, D.C. 20535-0001
www.nipc.gov/

The National Infrastructure Protection Center
investigates cyber crime carried out abroad,
and its web pages are a useful source of
further information on cyber crime.

US Department of Justice
10th & Constitution Ave., NW, Criminal
Division, (Computer Crime & Intellectual
Property Section), John C. Keeney Building,
Suite 600, Washington, D.C. 20530
www.cybercrime.gov

The US Department of Justice's cyber crime
pages have a wealth of information on the
issue, and how it is being fought.

Contacts in Australia and New Zealand

Australian Federal Police
Canberra City Police Station,
16/18 London Circuit,
Canberra City, ACT 2601
Tel: (61) 2 6245 7208
www.afp.gov.au/page

Information is available on the Australian
Federal Police's cyber crime strategy.

The Internet Safety Group
The Internet Safety Group, sponsored by the
New Zealand education department, offers
information on how to use the Internet safely,
and how the net is policed in New Zealand.
email: comments@netsafe.org.nz
www.netsafe.org.nz/

Further reading and viewing

BOOK
*Cybercrime: Law Enforcement, Security
and Surveillance in the Information Age,*
Douglas Thomas and Brian D. Loader
(Routledge, 2000)

VIDEO & DVD
Wargames (1984)
starring Matthew Broderick

Disclaimer
All the Internet addresses (URLs) given in this book
were valid at the time of going to press. However,
due to the dynamic nature of the Internet, some
addresses may have changed, or sites may have
changed or ceased to exist since publication. While
the author and Publisher regret any inconvenience
this may cause readers, no responsibility for any
such changes can be accepted by either the author
or the Publisher.

53

Glossary

browser
software for accessing websites and displaying web pages, e.g. MS Internet Explorer, Netscape

CERT
the Computer Emergency Response Team. A US government organization that tracks security incidents.

chatboard/chatroom
place on the Internet where you can 'chat', through your computer, with other people

constitution
set of important rules that say how a country should be run, and what rights should be protected

credit card
card from a credit card company authorizing the holder to buy goods on credit and pay for them later

defraud
to steal, often by lying, deceiving the victim or pretending to be someone else

denial of service attack
kind of cyber crime where computers, sometimes infected with a virus, send messages to one other computer on the Internet. Because the target receives so many messages, it may break down, meaning its real users stop being served.

e-commerce
the buying and selling of goods over the Internet

email
electronic messages sent over the Internet or over other computer networks

encryption
method of scrambling the conversations between computers so they would appear meaningless to anyone who attempted to listen in

firewall
machine and/or a piece of software that stops certain types of message getting into your computer from the Internet

fraud
theft, often by deceit (see defraud, above)

hacker
someone who enjoys using computers for a hobby, especially to gain unauthorized access to other people's computers

hard disk/hard drive
the big storage space on your computer

Internet
the worldwide computer network, which links up lots of other, smaller, computer networks

macro
small, easily-created computer program that carries out boring or repetitive tasks for you

MP3
kind of music file, which has been compressed (squashed) to make it easier to send over the Internet

network
collection of computers joined together so they can communicate with each other

online
you are online when your computer is connected to the Internet

personal computer (PC)
A personal computer is a computer small enough to fit on your desk. Once, all computers were much larger.

pirating
making copies of a piece of music, video or software without the copyright owner's permission

pornography
depiction of sexual activity in an unpleasant way

scam
scheme to defraud people

software
instructions that run your computer, often stored in your hard disk

treaty
agreement between countries to have the same law

virus
software program that spreads from machine to machine without the computer owner's permission

web server
software that runs a website. It manages all the web pages and handles requests from browsers to read pages.

World Wide Web
part of the Internet that is easy to move around and has special 'web browsing' software

Index